Anansi and Friends

poetry and prose by

Sally Huggins Toner

Finishing Line Press
Georgetown, Kentucky

Anansi and Friends

Copyright © 2019 by Sally Toner
ISBN 978-1-63534-978-8 First Edition
All rights reserved under International and Pan-American Copyright Conventions. No part of this book may be reproduced in any manner whatsoever without written permission from the publisher, except in the case of brief quotations embodied in critical articles and reviews.

ACKNOWLEDGMENTS

The Following pieces in this collection have appeared individually in other publications:

"Discovery" first appeared in *Postcard Poems and Prose*
"Anansi" first appeared in *Watershed Review*
"Lisa" first appeared in *Sky Island Journal*
"Slaughter Beach" and "Snow Duck on the Ides" appeared in a blog run by Silver Birch Press
"Snow Duck on the Ides" also appeared in *We are Residents Here*—an anthology from the 2018 Bridgewater International Poetry Festival

Publisher: Leah Maines
Editor: Christen Kincaid
Cover Art and Design: Sally Toner
Author Photo: Mark Toner

Printed in the USA on acid-free paper.
Order online: www.finishinglinepress.com
also available on amazon.com

Author inquiries and mail orders:
Finishing Line Press
P. O. Box 1626
Georgetown, Kentucky 40324
U. S. A.

Table of Contents

Discovery 1

Anansi 2

Slaughter Beach 4

Nettles 5

Snow Duck on the Ides 6

Lisa 7

Chemo Haikus 1-6 8

Surprise! (Caring Bridge Entry from April 13, 2017) 14

Chemo Haikus 7-9 21

Hamlet Tights 24

If You were the Woman, and I was the Man 25

I Want a New Birthday 27

The Reset Button (Caring Bridge Entry
    from September 1, 2017) 28

Additional Acknowledgments 34

Discovery

The bones were scattered
like jacks across the grass and leaves.
They were crime
half-buried, grime covered
and grey. My father
brought me here to hunt
for Christmas trees in
the ice-silent air

disturbed only by our steps
that sounded like
the crunch of fallen death,
or the passing
of a single engine plane
Cessna pilots love to fly,
the lonely drone that
won't leave me turbulence free.

Anansi

The trickster spider has appeared inside my flesh. She didn't exist just five months ago in the grey white ocean matter of the mammogram, with all its tributaries. But now her silk spirals out, a clump of mutant cells. She hid those months while I squeezed my nipple between my thumb and index finger, as I pressed and circled outward to check. Then, when she grew large enough, my husband found her, in an act of love that became a harbinger of death. Then they pressed her fresh fleshy home between two pieces of glass. The doctor showed her to me, a two centimeter spot of black. Twang, twang, that's the fly, the cells caught on the other side. She'll wrap them up and feed on them later, and then there may be another Anansi, then another, then another.

I didn't weep like I thought I would when they called with the diagnosis. If you really watch their faces, each health care professional looking increasingly concerned has a funny way of giving the news in stages. The oncologist doesn't give any numbers. "Staging cancer is so 1990s," she says. Numbers are for internet surfing before I take my pills that double as soldiers against nausea and anxiety. The oncologist and surgeon pass the baton and discuss my treatment options. We might outsmart her, Anansi, with chemicals—a pesticide to cut her web. Then a surgery and radiation to finish the job—broom sweeps to destroy the remnants. I don't need to surf the web to know it hurts.

My youngest daughter is 15. She is fearless, skipping along paths over cliffs during hikes in Maine and dodging lacrosse sticks at lightning speed. But the one thing she is terrified of is spiders, and I must introduce her to Anansi. Once, we had to wait an hour before we drove to school because she saw such an arachnid monster on the back of the passenger seat headrest. It was the size of a pencil eraser, ashen grey, black triangle on its back. I swiped it off like crumbs, and she screamed to wake the dead—pulled her knees to her chest, sucked her hands inside the frayed cuffs of her fuzzy sweater, and shook her head from side to side. Screaming, screaming, until I lied and said I'd found it, set it free. Back then, I believed harming Anansi would anger the gods. Now I know they're angry anyway. Or maybe they just don't care.

For now, I'll flutterpump my wings with all my might—race the salty girl before she scampers down my veins and lays her children. No, they won't be born. I shall raise my head and fist against the murderous mother, put the key in the ignition, and we'll all drive on.

Slaughter Beach

The water turns tar dark. They
lumber and lull, a thousand
mounds of spiky mud. Do their
tails hold poison? I never knew
in childhood, seeing
their crackling shells discarded.

Then I saw the ocean, up
the coast and up the years, a
home to ancient, alien lovers.
Their claws are zippered; the wife
lays eggs in a drying bed
while her husband twists in counterpoint.

Crabs are black sand thoughts, two part
Inventions. Some go home, retreating
with the waves or nudged
upright by my flip flop. Still,
the ones on shore, deposited
 too far for recovery—

They haunt me in the golden
mourning. Now, I walk,
silent along the scene—
a brined pile of failed rescue.
Their legs stiffen in the air, and
the stench makes me turn to take

a picture of a heron
on glass instead.

Nettles

Red dotting the shore, they looked like
nosebleeds that ran and spotted
my paper at school. I knew
the clear ones with nubs on their bellies were
safe—Popa chopped those for
bait. I hated no
water, building castles, dipping
buckets at the edge, pouring the
sea over my head with an eye out
for red.

So I'd go in anyway, lie on
my back, float in salt. Then I'd feel
one on my ankle, two
on my toes. I'd upright
myself, brush off razor
weeds, pack black sand on swelling
skin. I should've known
better. But of course
I forgot.
That's what children do.

Now, forewarned, I dive into
the pillow, thirsting for sleep. The stings
return as each hair brushes, falls
like tentacles from my toxic
scalp. I'm told it'll also hurt when
it grows back. As infants, we were wise
to nettles in all their forms. We knew what
would happen each time we went in
the water. Our eyes swam in brine,
remembering, forgetting, aware.

Snow Duck on the Ides

I see the stone creation, smaller than
my neuropathic hand. All thumbs, I stop
and fumble a shot. He's pocked, throat slit by sleet
and sun, but once upon a time his beak
was bright, the yellow of daffodils that cry
beside him. They're already dead, whether
cased in glass by weather or man.
The flowerpot man on the corner flashes
with flags on the fourth of July—a Santa hat
in December; when wind or rowdy kids
destroy, they fix him to resemble human
form again. The duck is different; his grief
 is real, compounded and ignored, like poison
in the veins until the statue, now
a stranger to himself, stares at me—
black spotted face reminding In a whisper
of precipitation, "I'm still here."

Lisa

Cloth covers rock and rubble over skin
and bone. We play a child's game, chasing
arrows around every corner to her
smile, humming Nat King Cole, I happen
to know she's been stolen and sold, had acid
and paint thrown on that face in front of mountains.
She hid at Chambord during the war. I wonder
when they lifted the blanket from her eyes,
did they dry like moth wings plastered to
the wall after a hard rain? Was she
relieved, resigned, sorry her locks stayed long
while other heads were shaved, their bodies fried?
She probably didn't give it a thought.
By then, she had already outlived us all.

Chemo Haiku #1

I brought a Big Mac
to chemo class fearing scorn.
I still passed. #Winning.

Chemo Haiku #2

Cow Cow Boogie while
the AC drips. Get hip, y'all.
Cassie, get along.

Chemo Haiku #3

My hair choked Fred, our
robot vacuum, so now my
Bitmoji goes cloche.

Chemo Haiku #4: On Getting Stuck

"You make a face," they
say. "It's okay," I laugh back.
"Anticipating."

Chemo Haiku #5: An Ode to AC

Not "The Red Devil"—
"Lady in Red." It takes a
bitch to beat a bitch.

Chemo Haiku #6: On a tired girl's obsession with HGTV

No tiny houses.
Home improvement? Give me a
hammer to smash walls.

Surprise!

Caring Bridge Journal Entry: April 13, 2017

Mark and I have six days to ourselves. Once-upon-a-time, we would have been doing the ebullient Homer Simpson, "WOOHOO" for the uninterrupted couple time. Yes, we're still enjoying our couple time. It's just that the cry this week is: "WOOHOO! SLEEP! WOOHOO! I CAN EAT PIZZA! WOOHOO! MY KNEE JOINTS STOPPED ACHING!"

The new regimen of Taxol had its possibility of a nasty allergic reaction, as I've written about previously. The infusion nurse was prepared, hooking extra adrenaline and major Benadryl to the IV pole in case I became Violet Beauregarde from Willy Wonka. Thankfully, I didn't. Two treatments of the new drug in, and it goes like this:

1. Sally cracks some jokes with Elli the infusion nurse as she flushes out her port.

2. Nurse Elli shows Sally the plastic bags of the good stuff and makes her identify her name and birthday.

3. Sally falls asleep as the Benadryl courses through her veins.

I am 3/4 through with the chemo, and I realize that I am behind in my Chemo Haikus. So I write Number Six, inspired by a conversation with a fellow infusion patient who has also become obsessed, recently, with HGTV.

I am still waiting for genetics results, thanks to a low white cell count when they took blood the first time. I should hopefully know something more by next week. An annoying surprise (a first cousin to "best laid plans") but not as bad as missing a treatment because of a super low count, landing in the hospital because of an infection, etc. Knock wood, I'm plugging along.

Speaking of wood, I am writing from a cabin chinked with oakum. Mark and I did take a little advantage of alone time to make a short spring break jaunt to Lone Fountain, Virginia to spend a couple of nights in one of our favorite places—the Hobson

House. This place, and its surprises, began for me a long time ago.

During my senior year in high school, I had the opportunity to complete a mentorship with a local professional. I had actually done one with a vet the year before, but my math grades had convinced me that STEM was not in my future, and, besides, I had kind of fallen in love with this writing thing by then. So I asked to be paired with a writer. Lee High hooked me up with a woman named Eve Hobson, who had just published a memoir about her experiences reporting, teaching, and living in British Columbia. The book was titled *Chinked with Oakum*. She lived in a log cabin in Lone Fountain, right outside of Churchville, about fifteen minutes from my house.

I remember pulling into her carport off Hanky Mountain Highway after snaking through a row of boxwoods, getting out of my used Buick, and being greeted at the door by a tall woman in her seventies with a shock of white hair, wearing bright blue eye shadow and a leopard print pantsuit.

"Well, helloooo," she said in the most amazing British accent. "You must be Sally. Come in!"

I had never encountered anyone like Eve Hobson in my seventeen years, and now I know I will never encounter anyone like her again. Nor will I ever step foot in a house like the one that belonged to her and her husband George.

The cabin is difficult to see from the road. You actually enter from what appears to be the side. In 1987, it was from the side that is now a locked kitchen for the B & B. Then, it was Eve's office. Today, guests enter from the other side.

Inside, the cabin is one large room, and one side of that room, with its four sides of picture windows, is floor to ceiling glass. When I first walked in, there were yellow legal pads covering every surface from desk to chair to the dining room table. A few minutes after I arrived, Eve's husband George walked down the carpeted spiral staircase from the second floor and greeted me as well. Bright blue eyes, a head of thick, curly white hair—one of the most attractive older men I had ever met. He soon excused himself to the yard where he was doing some maintenance. In my first afternoon at the Hobson House, I couldn't take my eyes off of those windows. There was a small pond with a running fountain off of the patio, then a larger pond in the distance. Later, when we walked outside, I was treated to the sound of the creek (eventually emptying into the Middle River, the same water source as Goshen Pass, one of my favorite spots down the road as a teen) about 100 yards from their back/front stoop. (With the design of the cabin, it's difficult to know, sometimes, which way is up. And that, I found, made it the PERFECT place for the Hobsons.)

A little more background on the Hobsons before I explain how we ended up back there this week (and every Easter break for about the last ten years). Eve was born in England at the turn of the century. In her late teens/early 20's, she immigrated to Australia with her first husband. They had a baby, prematurely, whom they lost. (She details all of this very matter-of-factly in *Chinked with Oakum*). She left Australia soon after and traveled to British Columbia, where she took various jobs from school van driver to teacher to journalist. She arrived ten minutes early for an interview with Richmond Hobson Jr, an adventure writer and son of Admiral Richmond Hobson, Spanish American War hero and captain of the Merrimack. Richmond wasn't ready to see her yet, but his brother, George, happened to answer the door. Which is why Eve said to her dying day that rule number one is to arrive at every appointment ten minutes early.

I never quite learned that lesson, but I'm still trying.

For Eve and George, it was, as hokey as this sounds, love at first sight. Their years in British Columbia are chronicled in Eve's memoir—their work, their love, their survival, and their cabin in the Canadian wilderness with a ram's head, Bumpy, above the hearth.

Sometime in the '50s, they decided to move, literally swirling their collective finger around a map and landing on Churchville, Virginia. They relocated and began breeding and selling Saint Bernards. One of the pens and the doggie doors are still visible from the yard. Eve proceeded to teach, get her Ph.D from UVA, and become, in her retirement, one of the premier literacy advocates in the Shenandoah Valley.

She was well retired by the time I met her in 1987. I had no idea that fall that she had already taught a dear friend, Sandy Kirtley, who would later become my first department chair at Wilson Memorial (my first teaching job). Sandy loves to tell the story of being in Eve's class when they learned of the Kennedy assassination.

"Someone came into the classroom and told us," Sandy says, "And Ms. Hobson stopped her lesson in the middle and asked all of us to get out our journals and begin writing. 'You need to record what you're feeling right now,' she said. 'Because, I, for one, have not been this shocked since Edward abdicated.'"

That was Eve. What else do I remember from the 30 hours I spent in my mentorship that fall? Her generosity in looking over and critiquing my writing. How much she obviously loved teaching. Her adorable husband. And that house. That house. All around the cabin were stones she'd plucked from the creek bed and painted with tempura. My favorite was an owl eye that still sits on the mantle as you walk in. Years later, when we began bringing our girls to the B & B, they took her cue, and we have multiple examples of their Hobson art around our townhouse today. One particular spring break, which fell early at the end of March, we got six inches of snow during our first day at the cabin. We had already played a long game of capture the flag in the snow, and I went upstairs to settle into an afternoon nap. When I woke up, Aimee had placed a painted rock by my bed. It was covered in a bright reddish orange, and she had copied words she had seen in our house before:

"And though she be but little, she is fierce."

Just one of the many surprises we've had in this magic place.

Oh, the explanation of how we got to come back nearly twenty years after I first crossed that threshold. Eve and George never had children of their own, but George had a son from a previous marriage, George Jr., nicknamed "Teeny." Eve writes of his visits to the cabin during the summers and of his gentle nature and burgeoning talent as a poet. Teeny is an Anglican priest, and a poet, who now lives in Paris. Both Eve and George lived into their nineties. After they died, Teeny apparently couldn't bring himself to sell the place. So he converted it into a B & B, keeping everything in the main house EXACTLY as it was when his parents lived there. Every book, every picture, every painted rock. The only things missing are the yellow legal pads. As my mother says, "It's like Eve and George just went out for a walk." My Dad happened to see the sign for the B & B in 2006 and inquired about it. He and mom, as a surprise, gave Mark and me two nights there for Christmas that year. So began our spring breaks at the Hobson House.

Let me explain. When I wrote my first novel in my early '30s—a YA concoction that still needs to be edited, I wrote about Eve, and that house. I explained to Mark that I had never met a person like her before or since and had also never fallen so immediately in love with a living space. To be able to walk back into that house over 20 years later...

Magic.

Every time we return, Eve shows me something else. One year, I found a collection of poems she wrote in her nineties. Yes, they were on yellow legal pad paper, and they were probably written from her upstairs bedroom because her osteoporosis was so bad at the end it was difficult for her to make it down those spiral stairs. Another year, it was a first edition of Thomas Hardy's *Jude the Obscure* tucked in one of the bookshelves in the guest room. (Hands off if you ever visit. It belongs to Eve.) This year, well, I'll get to that.

Eve is a true muse. You don't fully appreciate a person like her at 17, and there is no doubt that we have grown closer in the ten years I have been returning to her house, wandering, admiring her watercolors, her painted rocks, the vistas she set up—iron benches on every corner of the property. They've recently done some renovations—replaced the cedar roof and begun to repair a child's cabin with a tiny bed and desk, colored pencils, a potbellied stove. We were afraid at first that this meant Teeny is thinking of selling the cabin. Not yet, Pat the caretaker said. But he is, as she said, "Gettin' on. And you never know." The house is such a mixture of the aristocracy and the wild that created it. There are newspaper clippings about George's family, landed gentry from Alabama, framed and hanging on the wall, portraits of Eve's ancestors in thick gilded frames. And Bumpy the ram over the mantel as well as a bar proportionately huge for the size of the room with whiskey glasses hanging above it. The creek feeds the fountain, which bubbles up in all seasons. My mother likes to tell the story of one of her own visits to the house when she got the chance to do some volunteer work with Eve years after I had left home. George apparently greeted her at the door and proceeded to put on his knee length rubber boots to go out and unclog the fountain. They watched as he struggled. (The caretaker says they have constant trouble with the thing, but George and Eve were so proud of it.) Then the water began to spurt, and he ran into the house, still wearing his boots, caked with mud.

"EUREKA!" he shouted. "I DID IT."

My novel was fiction, but that scene definitely made it in.

The water from the creek feeds the fountain pond which then flows to the larger pond with the mallards and the swans. It seeps back into the earth and feeds the creek again, to the river, to the ocean.

And, I guess, eventually back to England, where Eve began.

So my surprise this time. Our first evening at the house, I woke up from a nap, and Mark and I went for a walk down by the creek. I always stare at the ground, scanning for wishing stones, those with rings of marble around their bellies. It was the time of magic light, and

I snapped a picture of the stream, enjoying the Zen of its sound. Then I looked behind me. Scratched into a boulder along the creek bed were these words:

"Don't give up!"

Then I looked at my feet, and there was a stone with a piece of weed, sundyed to a light pink, curved in the shape of a breast cancer ribbon.

I'm not even kidding.

"Well, Eve," I said, "I mean, I know I have chemo brain and all, and you wanted to make sure I got the message, but you could have been a LITTLE subtler. I haven't COMPLETELY lost my sense of metaphor."

She never stops surprising me.

Don't worry, Eve. I'm listening.

Chemo Haiku #7: In honor of a mentor gone, but not…

For this chemo girl
warmth runs from Hobson Pond through
my heart to the sea.

Chemo Haiku #8: For Mark

Sit; love this shrunken
hairless me no differently
than ever. Thank you.

Chemo Haiku #9

Ring that bell, sister!
Be still, take in that warped view,
clear like ancient stars.

Hamlet Tights

I have a tragedy inked
on my legs. No, you're not
stoned. That's the text of
Hamlet, covered with a
sweater, capped with black
lace combat boots—an extra
piercing, hair that flares so
everyone's aware of
my presence.

"Your eyes pop!" friends say, or
"You're such a badass!"
"An inspiration!"
"God bless."
Thank you
but

I fear a dearth of
miracles. Verses on
my legs, ruminations on
my purpose may sound
smart, but they're a ruse. This cowardly
 lioness finds her mind—wizardless.

Hand me Hamlet's
sword. I'm trained in the art
of self defense, but that was always just
attrition. In this time, in this state of
my union, I need more than
abstract nouns.

If You were the Woman, and I was the Man

I'd watch you undress, watch
you tie the gown across your
chest, pink rose petals over
breasts I can't bring myself
to touch—a scar I haven't
asked to see.

I would have planted other
flowers before—real roses
white ones—your favorite that
mated with others to make a
paler pink we'd walk by
after this appointment.

I'd curse the
conversation falling
to dirt, crushed with
leaves at
our
feet.

When you explain the trigger
of being alone is not your
greatest fear, when you plead
"Promise me you'll give
your need, even if the problem's
me—"

If you were the woman, and I was the man—

the words, "I'm.
Fine." would be armless
iron hands around your
throat. I'd remember
another mating, where
my discovery started this.

I'd feel as helpless as
the day the doctor's
call broke the
news, broke our
hearts, me unable to ask for
a Goddamned thing.

I Want a New Birthday

There's a goatfish in the stars today.
This day that found me lost a year
ago. Now, an anniversary
of well. Then, a diagnosis.
Today we drink champagne.
So why can't I change my sign?

I want a new birthday.

Their hybrid babes may bleat and
bray, but all I'll say is Capricorn is where
it's at. I want to crawl from sea
to land. I'm through with Pisces
sensitivity. Head
butting for the win, that's me!

I used to need the surf to
breathe and had to jump so high above
the waves to glimpse the sun. I dodged
the hook and scraped the barnacles
from my skin on coral only to be gutted
in the end.

Now, I'll be born in the dawn of
the year with hair that's coarse and devil's
horns. I'll hobble the farm, a genius
klutz, scarfing other people's
garbage, turning it to milk. I'll slip
under fences. Don't forget

These goats can swim, if they must.

The Reset Button
Last entry from the Caring Bridge Journals —September 1, 2017

Kasey, the nurse from the radiation oncologist's office, called me this evening. I sat in my car, parked in the cul-de-sac after I dropped Sara and her field hockey teammate off at her mom's house to do some homework.

"Hello, Ms. Toner. When you left the office on Tuesday, I know the doctor mentioned a follow-up visit in a month, but I don't recall scheduling one with you. I know it's a little trickier now with your teaching schedule, but would you like to do that now?..."

Gee, did I forget to stop by the front desk and compare calendars when I have been visiting this office every day for the past five weeks and really, more than anything, wanted to do my very best Road Runner impression after they sprung me from the isotopic massage table?

Meep meep.

"Sure, Kasey. What works for you?"

In truth, they have all been more than wonderful. There was the day when Hope, one of the nurses, had Motown's greatest hits ready for me before I even named my walkup song. Funny, though, they didn't ask me what it was on my last day.

"Na na na na, na na na na...hey hey hey...goodbye."

Three words...

I am done.

Yes, there are follow-ups to come. And a good deal of time looking over my shoulder. My hair still needs to move from Chia Pet status to something a little more deliberate. My oncologist says that, while we recover to about 80% within two months after chemo, it takes about a year to get back to 100%.

But...

I am done.

"Is that gunk out of your system?" a former student asked via Facebook tonight. And my first thought was actually chemo.

"I mean the cancer," she said.

That's the thing. As you're going through treatment, and dealing with how sick it makes you, it's easy to forget why you're doing all of this in the first place. Cassandra is toast. She has been, for a while. As I said in a poem, "a crater of scar in this bald body."

The gunk is gone.

I am done.

But there will still, sometimes, be ticks.

I got another call today, this one from our oldest daughter. She's volunteering at a camp for children with parents who have cancer, spending her week with a cabin of 6-8 year-old-girls with some unfathomable stories, teaching them the therapeutic value of painting. I am beyond proud of her. She was a little freaked out because, when she took off her bathing suit this afternoon, she found six ticks on her stomach.

I would have been hysterical in this situation. My first born apologized for interrupting my planning period.

We'll go through the protocol, look for the rash, get a prescription for antibiotics, keep our fingers and toes crossed. Lyme is no joke. But she found these suckers really quickly, and her cabin mates checked her back and her hair. She's done all she can.

She'll be okay. And so will we all.

But there will always be those tiny parasitic fears, nagging doubts, feelings of anger, guilt, regret that burrow into our flesh and, if we let them stay there, become engorged. If we don't acknowledge them, pluck them out carefully, they inject their venom. They make us sick. Still, there's no way to avoid them. That would mean never going outside, always avoiding the tall grass. That's where adventure lives. It would be sad to travel only on the paved roads.

But where the tall grass lives, so do the ticks.

The good news is that my first born took a nice hot shower, had her cabinmates check her over again, and reminded herself that she will, by this time tomorrow night, be back in the city, ready to press the reset button.

That's what I'd like to end with. The reset button.

I remember a book club meeting years ago where we discussed the novel *Water for Elephants*. (a fantastic read if you haven't gotten the chance.) There is so much that happens to the young protagonist, a transformation, love, loss, redemption…and it all takes place in the span of a year. So my question to the women in this group was, "Think of a year that transformed you—365 days that you consider a 'reset button' on your world view, your self view, your lives."

It was one of the coolest discussions I've ever had. Each of us talked about an experience, a place and time, that continues to travel with us, for good and for bad. I've had family members talk about how glad I must be to have treatment "in the rearview mirror." I am, more than you can imagine. The past eight months is shorter than what so many have to endure, but it's certainly enough. I'm loving being able to taste food again. Imagine what it's like feeling like every meal you eat is the best one you've had in a year? I've had several "best meals" in the past few weeks, which tells me that I'm catching up on that last 20 percent. I'm tired, but I'm also starting the school year. I want to click my heels when I still have the energy to stop by the grocery store on the way home. I look at pictures of myself from February and March and hardly recognize that person. It seems like much much longer than a few months ago. There is much in the rearview mirror. And I am so grateful.

Still, the past eight months won't disappear. They have transformed me, hopefully in good ways more than bad. The night I was diagnosed, a friend told me the things I would learn through all of this. She's a master teacher, so that reaction on her part made total sense.

"You'll learn how to be still," was the last thing she said. And she was so right. As a child, I was much better at that. There was this activity record, *Having Fun with Ernie and Bert,* that I used to listen to incessantly. Mom still talks about how she would walk by my room and see me lying on the floor following Jim Henson's (as Ernie) instructions on how to imagine. Guided visualization, I'd learn much later in my education classes. In fact, the song "Here in the Middle of Imagination" is still my favorite Sesame Street song.

"...I look inside, and discover things that are sometimes strange and new, and the most remarkable thoughts I think, have a way of being true..."

Being still. It has its place. Time for imagination, time for meditation, time for prayer.

Time to let the reset button do its thing.

There are things you lose when you reset. Some files get lost, corrupted. I have scars on both sides of my body that will always remind me of Cassandra, a dark patch of skin above my heart the radiation oncologist says will fade but may never completely go away. I lost a couple of inches from not eating for a while (that I wouldn't mind staying lost...).

What have I gained? More like regaining that ability to lie on the floor and let my imagination take over. I still have a temper, but maybe I've learned to use moments of still, moments of pause, to gauge my reactions to things I cannot control.

There is, of course, an appreciation for every day I'm granted. More than that, though, there's this appreciation of PEOPLE we're granted that I thought I had, but now...people can be small, and cruel, downright shitty. Evil even. But they are also our greatest gifts. That's what I told my oldest yesterday afternoon when she was talking about the kids she's been with in the past week—their grief and fear that is much more alarming than the physical bugs she pulled off her skin. There is grief. There is fear. There is evil.

But there is also love.

"Those kids and your time together is a gift to you, Aimee," I said. "And you are a gift to them." I've been thinking a lot about appreciating people as the school year has started. Working with teenagers all day can be challenging. Still, wow...in the end...every one of those 100+ people I get to spend time with every day. What a gift.

I hope I can express that to them throughout the year. I hope I can express my appreciation to everyone in my life a little better than I have. That's a goal I have gained from this. Gained from my moments of still.

There will be other years of transformation. (I'm so grateful for that too.) When I picked up the younger daughter, we took a driving lesson, pulling onto Wiehle Avenue, our street. It also happens to be a terrifying road—a thoroughfare to a metro stop, where people pull around a blind corner way too fast. Once a month, we hear an accident or near accident from our kitchen window. When I told Sara we were going on Wiehle, her eyes grew wide.

"Whhat? Are you sure?"

"You have to do it sometime. But we don't have to if you don't want to tonight."

"No, I'm ready."

We pulled out of her friend's neighborhood and used the green arrow to turn onto the street. A motocycle whizzed by on our left; the guy was actually standing on his foot rests. Sara made a noise but never flinched.

She drove me home, and she did a beautiful job.

"How did it feel?" I asked after she pulled into the parking space. She just smiled.

Reset, move forward.

And let the story go on.

Additional Acknowledgements

This is a book about illness, and recovery—about a 2.5 centimeter clump of growing cells that invaded my body, and our home, in the winter of 2017. She's no longer with us, but she had multiple names. One of those names, Anansi, was one I used for a piece that started, years ago, as fiction—that nightmare I brought to the front of my brain so it wouldn't end up being real. I found out that doesn't always work. The tumor's other name, Cassandra, was part mythology, part pink shrinking dragon from a children's show.

My therapy during treatment was much of the poetry and prose you will find in this book. As I write this introduction, two years out from chemo, with a full head of hair and a much stronger body, some of this work, like pictures of me during that time, is almost unrecognizable. But here it is, nevertheless, written, revised, reflected upon.

My thank-yous begin with a quote from the last piece in this collection— my last Caring Bridge journal entry after completing radiation:

There is, of course, an appreciation for every day I'm granted. More than that, though, there's this appreciation of PEOPLE we're granted that I thought I had, but now...people can be small, and cruel, downright shitty. Evil even. But they are also our greatest gifts.

I want to say thank you, in particular, to my three greatest gifts. First, to my husband, Mark. You are my best friend and, in every sense of the word, a lifesaver. Je t'aime. Always.

And to my daughters, Aimee and Sara—their father would agree so much greater than the sum of their parts. You are our heroes. As I told you that January night, this is a wonderful life, and I'm going to continue to fight like hell to keep and make the most of it. Thank you for being the best reason of all for doing that.

Sally Toner has lived and taught high school English in the Washington, D.C., area for over twenty years but hails from every corner of the state of Virginia. With family ties to Abingdon that go back centuries to Tidewater to the Shenandoah Valley, the ocean, the mountains, and the tease of Mid-Atlantic seasons, literal and figurative, have had a profound influence on her work.

She earned a BA in English and a minor in music from the College of William and Mary in 1992 and married a year later, eventually putting down roots in the original planned community of Reston, where she lives with her husband and two daughters (when they aren't up north in school or driving to the practice field around the corner). She is a three-time runner-up in the F. Scott Fitzgerald fiction contest sponsored by Montgomery College and a winner of the prize for literary non-fiction in the F. Scott Fitzgerald Photojournalism Competition sponsored by the University of Baltimore. Her work has appeared in *Gargoyle* magazine, *The Delmarva Review, Watershed Review*, and other publications. Her fiction is also included in *Defying Gravity*—a collection of work from Washington, D.C., area women writers edited by Richard Peabody. *Anansi and Friends* is her first published collection.

www.ingramcontent.com/pod-product-compliance
Lightning Source LLC
LaVergne TN
LVHW041559070426
835507LV00011B/1195